GW00870220

Tchi pitchi

What a pity

and Other Jèrriais Phrases

Jo Olszewski and Tracy Peters

This book is a result of weekly Jèrriais sessions, chatting in the
Adelphi Pub in St. Helier, Jersey, Channel Islands

First published in 2020

Copyright © Jo Olszewski and Tracy Peters
Cover design and illustrations by © Cosmo Mulford

ISBN 9798614758479

For all those friends who have ever wondered out loud what to do on a rainy Tuesday evening…

Contents

Foreword

Foreword

Most phrase books aim to help you converse with the locals, but in Jersey you won't hear much of the approximately 1,000 year old language being spoken.

That said, it is still visible, which is why it's puzzling when people state that Jèrriais is dead and useless. It's usual to hear people say that they are taking the kids to *Grève* or *Les Mielles*, and that they live near a *cotil* or are cutting their hedge for *Branchage* – these useful Jèrriais words describe the diverse geological and cultural nature of the island.

This book is not intended as 'an academic analysis of language.'* We want to share with you the increased understanding that Jèrriais has given us of our chosen island. This colourful language, with its descriptive place names and phrases, is useful when travelling around the island and to comment on daily life – often in exasperation. We have added handy tips for pronunciation, just in case. After all, any language with a plethora of phrases for being drunk and an insult that describes someone as having 'a face like a roasted cat' has got to be worth investigating!

This descriptive, inventive, metaphorical language never ceases to amaze us. However, some expressions and insults (p28-31) are probably not suitable family reading around the table at tea-time. Therefore, we have categorised these as 'those you can use in company', 'those you can throw over your shoulder then walk away' and those 'best muttered under your breath or replayed in your own head', in order to let you decide when to skip bits.

We are grateful to Cosmo Mulford for his artwork and indebted to Geraint Jennings, who remains our guru…and a national treasure.

*While our intentions are not academic, neither do we decry those who wish to investigate the language from a less 'tongue in cheek' standpoint. Therefore, if you are looking for a more detailed account of the language, we suggest the following publications and authorities:

Le Jèrriais Pour Tous by Paul Birt, available at the Société Jersiaise
Dictionnaithe Angliais / Jèrriais and Jèrriais / Angliais available at the Société Jersiaise
L'Office du Jèrriais, www.jerriais.org.je
Jersey Heritage, www.jerseyheritage.org

Pronunciation

Key to pronouncing your Jèrriais words

Now, the French settlers sometimes encountered difficulty ascribing letters to sounds they heard in Jèrriais; hence they used 'qu' to represent the sound 'ch', as in 'church'. These days, those who know Jersey will know that Les Quennevais sports centre is pronounced with an English 'k' at the beginning (not the 'qu' sound as in 'queen'). However, back in the day, these initial letters were pronounced as 'ch' (as in 'church').

We have used a phonetic-style system that relates to the speech sounds to try to help you learn how to pronounce these Jèrriais words.

Though the international phonetic alphabet is standard for such exercises we chose not to use it for fear of inducing brain-ache in those unfamiliar with it!

We have included a key to assist in pronunciation because you can't always tell how something sounds from the way that it is spelt. Our example above of the sports centre would be written in our pronunciation key as *Lai chen-vai*.

Hey look, if you're finding this confusing, don't give up – you can be pretty successful in your pronunciation fairly easily and that is good enough for us.

Pronunciation Key

Spelling	Pronunciation	Example of how this sounds
oo	oo	As in h**oo**t
oh	oa	As in b**oa**t
u	uh	As in **uh**?
ai	ai	As in tra**i**tor
ch	ch	As in **ch**erry
sh	sh	As in **sh**ut up
a	a	As in m**a**d
ss	s	As in hi**ss**
s	z	As in shoe**s**
je	zh	As in Dr. **Zh**ivago
j	j	As in **J**aws
(n)	(short) n	A nasal sound where you are left with an open mouth (attractive, huh?) As in saying 'bring', but not quite finishing the word.
k	k	As in **c**at
aa	ar	As in p**a**rt

r	r	As in run. In fact, where 'r' is written, you should pronounce it, as they do in the West Country in England
a	a	As in cat
o	o	As in Tom
w	w	As in water
ee	ee	As in bee
th	th	As in bathe
e	e	As in pet
i	i	As in pit

Parishes

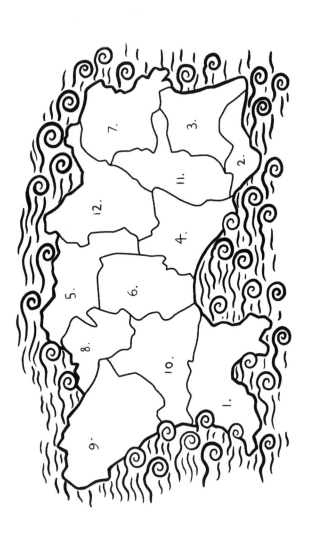

Parishes, Parishioners and their Nicknames

Where do you live? Whom do you visit?

1. Les Carpéleuses – [Lai Kaar-pel-uhz] The Caterpillars.

2. Enfeutchi – [On-fur- chee] Full of Smoke, likely to be due to the burning of vraic (a type of seaweed) in the area.

3. Enfeutchi – Also Full of Smoke, likely to be due to the burning of vraic (a type of seaweed) in the area. The smoke must have travelled a long way!

4. Les Clyichards – [Lai Kee-shaar] Unfortunately, The Shitters, due to the prevalence of dysentery in town. As you will see, Jèrriais is a very direct and descriptive language!

5. Les Nièrs Tchus – [Lai Ny-er- choo] The Black Arses, perhaps due to the boggy mud they sat in to produce flax cloth.

6. No nickname.*

7. Les Nordgiens – [Lai Nor-j(n)] The Northeners.

8. Les Rouôlots – [Lai Roh-loh] The Roly-Polys and also Les Bourdélots – [Lai - Bord – e- loh], possibly because they ate lots of sweet rolled buns. A Bourdélot is a cored apple baked with spices encased in pastry. Give it a go!

9. Les Gris Ventres – [Lai Gree Vo(n)-tr] The Grey Bellies, named after the grey wool produced in that area.

10. Les Ventres Baînis – [Lai Vo(n)-tr bai-nee] The Limpet Bellies, maybe because they enjoyed their limpet stew.

11. No nickname.*

12. Les Nordgiens - [Lai Nor-j(n)] also The Northeners. They travelled a long way!

* As numbers 6 and 11 do not appear to have had nicknames, we will propose Les Acateurs dé Livres: 'The Book Buyers', and live in hope!

Speaking

The Basics

Hint – In Jèrriais 'dg' makes a 'j' sound, as in Jersey and 'l' after a
consonant makes a 'y' sound, as in 'yellow'

Jèrriais	English	Pronunciation
Oui	Yes	Wee
Oui-dgia!	Yes indeed	Wee-ja
Nânnîn	No	No-na(n)
S'i' t'pliaît	Please	Ssee t pee-yai
Mèrcie bein des fais	Thank you very much	Muh-ssee ban de fai
Jé n'comprends pon	I don't understand	Zhen co(n)-pra(n) po(n)

Saying Hello

In Jèrriais 'ou' followed by a vowel makes a 'w' sound, as in St.Ouen in the North West of Jersey and for French speakers, the same sound as in 'Oui'.

Jèrriais	English	Pronunciation
Bouônjour	Hello	Bwon-zhaw
Bouônjour à matîn	Good morning	Bwon-zhaw a mata(n)
Bônsouair	Good evening	Bon sswear

Carrying on the Hellos

In Jèrriais a 'd' followed by an apostrophe rarely makes any noise.

Jèrriais	English	Pronunciation
Comme est qu'tu'es?	How are you?	Kom ai ke-too wai?
J'sis d'charme	I'm fine	Zhe-ssee dshaam
Comme unne vyi	Like an old man	Kom un vee
Comme eune vielle	Like an old woman	Kom oon vyel
Comme lé temps	Like the weather	Kom le ton

Saying Goodbye

Jèrriais	English	Pronunciation
À bi!	Bye!	Abee
À la préchaine	Till next time	A la prai-shan
Bouonne niet	Goodnight	Bwon n-yai
Bouôn viage!	Bon voyage!	Bwon vi-ya-zh

Expressions of Insult and Exasperation

Come on, who learns the rudiments of a language and doesn't want to know the naughty words?

So here we give you expressions that you can happily throw around when annoyed and when in company. The 'over-the-shoulder and walk away' insults and the expressions best muttered under your breath or replayed in your own head. There are the frankly bizarre ones and we show you the little gems you'll wish you'd known all your life: these are often 'of their time' and speak of the Jersey way of life perfectly.

In Company

Jèrriais	English	Pronunciation
Né m'emm'luque d'aut'!	Stop bugging me!	Nem om-look doht!
Nou n'y comprend ni tchu ni tête	You can't make arse or head out of it (you can't make head nor tail of it)	Noo ni com-pro(n) ni choo ni tait
Pouôrre boûse d'âne!	Poor donkey turd!	Pwor booz daan!

Ch'est comme amouoch'ler du sablion	It's like piling up sand (a waste of time)	Shai com am-wash-lai doo sa-bio(n)
Les mauves sont affrontées comme un bélet	The seagulls are as cheeky as a weasel	Lai mohv-zon afron-tai com un bel-et
Cârre-té!/cârr'-ous!	Get out of the way! (to one person/to a group)	Car tai / car-oo!
Belle débâte!	Good riddance!	Bel de-baat!
Sâbre dé bouais et pistolet d'pânnais!	Cripes! Jeez! Literally – wooden sword and parsnip pistol (yes, we know!)	Saa-br dai bwai ai pisto-la dpaan-nai!

Over Your Shoulder and Walk Away

Jèrriais	English	Pronunciation
Péter pus haut qu'san tchu	To be full of yourself (literally, fart higher than your arse)	P-te poo hoo-k san choo
Baîse man tchu	Kiss my arse	Base mon choo
Un couochon*	A pig	U(n) kwo-shon

*You may not be offended but believe me, in Jèrriais terms, reference to a pig is bad! So much so, in fact, we have devoted a whole section (p.43) to the pinkish farm animal with a snout, highlighting ways to speak about a pig, without saying 'pig'!

Under Your Breath or in Your Head

Jèrriais	English	Pronunciation
Fou pas d'ma dgeule!	F**k off	Foo paa d-ma jel
Fouaitheuse!	S**t head! (f)*	Fwoo-ai-thes!
Fouaitheux!	S**t head ! (m)*	Fwoo ai-thwe!
Tu pense qué tu'es pus haut qu'un tchu d'un tchian	You think that you are higher than a dog's arsehole How much more satisfying is this than our equivalent: 'You've got ideas above your station!?'	Too pons k too ai poo hoe kan choo dun chon

*Yes, even in such stressful times as when you might be tempted to use this insult, you must remember whether you are insulting a male or a female.

Just Bizarre

Jèrriais	Il a eune barbe d'gardîngni, nou pouôrrait tchier entre les brîns
Pronunciation	Il a oon barb d'gardain-nee; noo pwoo-rai chi-ai ont-tr lai bra(n)
Translation	He's got a gardener's beard; you could shit between the hairs
Jèrriais	N'y'a rein d'pus emmèrdant qu'un emmèrdément tch'emmèrde!
Pronunciation	Nya rand poo emerd-ant kun emer-dai-mon cho-merd!
Translation	There's nothing more bloody annoying than a bloody annoying annoyance!
Jèrriais	V'là tchi cadre comme un couochon en manchettes!
Pronunciation	Vla chi kaadr com un kwo-shon on mon-shet!
Translation	It is like a pig in sleeves!
Jèrriais	Eune minne dé cat rôti
Pronunciation	Oon min duh kar roaw-tee
Translation	To have a face like a roasted cat

Little Gems

Jèrriais	Un pithot coêffi
Pronunciation	Un pitho cway-fee
Translation	Hoity toity
Literal Translation	A goose wearing the lace headdress

Jèrriais	J'ai des freumions
Pronunciation	Zhay dai frem-ee-o(n)
Translation	I've got pins and needles
Literal Translation	I've got ants

Jèrriais	Ch'est piéthe qu'à féther des mouques
Pronunciation	She pyeth ka fai-the dai mook
Translation	It is worse than putting horse shoes on a fly

Jèrriais	Ch'est comme touos les pithots du mathais tchi caqu'tent
Pronunciation	She com t-woa lai pi-thoa doo mat-hai chee kukt
Translation	What a racket
Literal Translation	It is like all the geese in the marsh nattering

Jèrriais	Envyer des pouèrs
Pronunciation	On vee-yai dai pwe-r
Translation	To curse someone
Literal Translation	To send someone lice

Jèrriais	l'craît en bas comme la coue d'eunne vaque
Pronunciation	Ee-crai on baa kom la koo doon vak
Translation	He is short
Literal Translation	He grows down like a cow's tail

Jèrriais	D'la grôsse lédgeunmes
Pronunciation	Dla grohss le-jumz
Translation	Big heads
Literal Translation	Big veg

Jèrriais	Un rat dans la gorge
Pronunciation	Un ra don la gorzh
Translation	To have a croaky voice
Literal Translation	To have a rat in the throat

Jèrriais	Nou n'trouve pon les sou pitchis au bu des ronches
Pronunciation	Noon troov po(n) lai soo pich-ee o boo dai ronsh
Translation	Money doesn't grow on trees
Literal Translation	You don't find money stuck on the end of brambles

Jèrriais	Dé l'hielle dé pid d'moûque
Pronunciation	De yel de peed mook
Translation	Elbow grease
Literal Translation	Oil of the fly's foot

Jèrriais	La machinne-chouette
Pronunciation	La mash-in shwet
Translation	Thingamabob

Jèrriais	Il a l'beurre touônné au bouôn bord
Pronunciation	Il a le ber two-nai o bwon bor
Translation	All right for some
Literal Translation	He has got the butter on the right side

Jèrriais	l'finnitha ès tchians
Pronunciation	Ee fini-tha ai chon
Translation	He will end up going to the dogs/destitute

Jèrriais	Oulle est sale, oulle cliut'tait ès pathais
Pronunciation	Ool-e sal, ool-e kyoo-tai e pa-thai
Translation	It is so dirty that it would stick to the wall

Jèrriais	Êt' au rouoyaume des taupes
Pronunciation	Ait o rwo-yem dai top
Translation	To be dead
Literal Translation	To be in the kingdom of the moles

Jèrriais	Souos les mèrgots
Pronunciation	Swo-lai mer-go
Translation	To be dead
Literal Translation	Under the daisies

Words from a Way of Life

In a community where the land and the sea (and social gaiety to match hard work) were so important, many words and expressions developed around these themes.

The Farm

Working the land, getting goods to market, knitting Jerseys, making cider and drinking cider(!) was a way of life. (A 'thank you' should be extended here to General Don for his road construction exercise in the early 1800s; before this, getting goods to market was an extremely difficult task – you can see his commemorative statue in Parade Gardens, St. Helier today.)

Jèrriais	English	Pronunciation
Laisse paître et coucous	To leave to pasture	Laiss paitr ai koo-kooss
Tchéthue	To plough	Chai-thoo
Un côti (m) (n)	A sloping patch of land	U(n) Koht-ee
Un pithot	A goose	U(n) pith-oh
Un picot	A turkey/dot/ point	U(n) pik-oh
Un vaque	A cow	U(n) vok

Un cat	A cat	U(n) kot
Un tchian	A dog	U(n) chon
Un j'va	A horse	U(n) zhva
Un mouc à mie	A bee (literally, a honey fly)	U(n) mook a mee
Un vers de terre	An earthworm	U(n) vair de tir
Un crapaud	A toad	U(n) Krap-oh
Un pommyi	An apple tree	U(n) pom-yee
Eune brèbis	A sheep	Oon bre-bee
Un tchoeur	A cherry	U(n) chur
Un tcherier	A cherry tree	U(n) che-ree-ai

That Pinkish Farm Animal with a Snout

In Jèrriais, it is considered extremely uncouth to refer to this particular farm animal by its correct title – especially in the presence of a lady – and so euphemisms developed as a solution:

Jèrriais	English	Pronunciation
Un ketteau/ quetôt	A pig	U(n) ke-toh
Un ket	A pig	U(n) ket
Un Bête à sé	A pig	U(n) bait a sai
Un vêtu à sé	A pig	Un vait-oo a sai
Un petit bonhomme	A pig	U(n) pet-ee bon-om
Un petit monsieur	A pig	U(n) pet-ee mon-syer
Un avé	A pig/child	U(n) av-ai
Rêver la rouoge trie et l'nièr couchon	To have a nightmare (literally to dream of the red sow and black pig)	Rai-ver la rwoozh tree ai l-nyer kwo-shon
Li'tait pliein coumme un quétot	Drunk as a pig	Lai-tai pyee-en kom u(n) ke-toh

The Sea

For the fishermen and beach-combers alike. Limpet stew anyone?

Hint – the circumflex (punctuation mark that looks like a hat) extends the vowel sound….

Jèrriais	English	Pronunciation
La mé	The sea	La mai
Eune caûchie	Harbour	Oon koh-shee
Un port	Bay, inlet	U(n) por
Un bâté pêtcheux	Fishing boat	U(n) baa-tai pet-shuh
La mathée	Tide	La math-ai
Les baînis	Limpets	Lai Bain-ee
Un Mechot	A razor fish	U(n) mai-shoh
Hapé un paîsson	To catch a fish	Hap-ai u(n) pai-sson
Les mauves	Seagulls	Lai mohv

Drinking

Work hard, play hard, have lots of words for the end result....

Jèrriais	English	Pronunciation
L'auberge	The pub	Loh-berzh
As-tu sé?	Are you thirsty?	A too sai?
Té pliaît-ti'à baithe?	Would you like a drink?	T pee-ai ti a bev?
Santé	Cheers	Son-tai
J'sis p'lé d'sé	I'm very thirsty	Zh-see plai dssai
Ch'est té tchi convyie	It's your round	Shai tai chee kon-vyee
Craûler	To swagger, sway	Kroh-lai
Il'tait plein coumme un ticlyie	He was a drunk as a kettle	Itai plen kom u(n) tee-klai
Bastant	Tipsy	Bas-tant
Un trop-pliein	A drunk man	U(n) troh-pyen

Eune biche	A drunk woman	Oon beesh
A maintchi pliein	Half drunk	A man-chee pyen
Bragi	Drunk	Brag-ee
Chonme	Drunk	Shohm
Gris	Drunk	Gree
Gaté d'bethe	Drunk	Gatai dbeth
Blinde	Drunk	Blind
Rousse	Drunk	Rooz
Soûl	Drunk	Sool
Pliein	Drunk	Pyen

You get the picture!

Places

Places

"I don't know any Jèrriais." Well, good, thon you might buy this book, but we have to let you into secret...The following are generic, but may also be familiar to you.

Jèrriais	English	Pronunciation
Un portélet	A cove	U(n) port-let
Un hâvre	An inlet that can have an anchor	U(n) haavr
Eune grève	A beach	Oon grev
Les mielles	The sand dunes	Lai mi-yel
Les Quennevais	The hemp fields	Lai chen-vai
La p'tite maîson	The toilet	La p-teet mai-zon
Un moulîn	A windmill, watermill	Un moo-lan
Eune falaise	A cliff	Oon fal-aiz
D'Azette	Place of rest	Da-zet
Eune cache	A drive	Oon kash
Un côti	A steep sloping field	U(n) koh-tee
Eune hougue	A mound	Oon hoog
Mal / mau	Bad	Mal / moh

Specific Places

Take this book on a journey around the island and look out for the following:

Place Name	La Route Orange St. Brelade
English	Orange Road
Where/Why?	Jean Orange was the Connétable (Constable) of St. Brelade from 1820-1826. For those of you not familiar with the system; each Parish elects a Constable to look after its affairs for three years.
Place name	Rue de Maupertuis St. Clement
English	Smelly/bad orifice road
Where/Why?	Probably so named because of a malodorous bog nearby – at that time.

Place name	La Grande Route Des Sablons Grouville
English	The main road of sand
Where/Why?	In Jèrriais sablier is sand and indeed Sand Street in St. Helier was also originally called Rue des Sablons, reflecting what it would have looked like before reclamation of land began.
Place name	Rue de Dèrrière St. Helier
English	The road behind
Where/Why?	King Street (take a close look at the street sign). This was not the main High Street in Jersey, but the road behind it, which mainly contained the backyard gates of properties in Broad Street at one time.

Place name	Rue (de) Trousse-Cotillons St. Helier
English	Holding up Petticoats Road
Where/Why?	Where ladies hoisted their petticoats in order to avoid soiling them with the muck prevalent in Royal Square, which was a typical market place of that time.
Place name	Rue de la Planque Billot St. Helier
English	Mr Billot's plank of wood Road
Where/Why?	York Street. Mr Billot placed that plank in a particularly muddy place in order to assist crossing – what a gent!
Place name	Rouge Bouillon St. Helier
English	Red spring
Where/Why?	Due to the red soil and bubbling springs, now paved over, but you still might still spot crapauds (toads) in the gardens on a rainy night.

Place name	La Colomberie St. Helier
English	The dove cote
Where/Why?	Where the Seigneur (VIP) of the parish kept his doves as a supply of meat.

Place name	La Pouquelaye St. Helier
English	The Dolmen
Where/Why?	In Jèrriais this read 'La Pouclée' but, as with many place names, it has been anglicised. There was once a megalithic tomb (dolmen) in this location.

Place name	Les Chénolles St. John
English	Crank handle
Where/Why?	The road is winding and resembled the shape of a crank handle. These were commonly used to start engines (think Chitty Chitty Bang Bang!)
Place name	La Rue des Varvots St. Lawrence
English	Road of mud or the lavoir
Where/Why?	A lavoir was a natural water source where people washed their clothes.

Place name	Le Saut Geffroy St. Martin
English	Jeffrey's Leap
Where/Why?	Folklore has it that this is where criminal Geffroy (Jeffrey) was sentenced to be thrown into the sea. Amazingly Geffroy survived and swam back to shore. Whilst the crowd argued about what should happen to him, Geffroy brashly offered to repeat his amazing feat. Unfortunately, this time he knocked his head on a rock and was killed. The moral of this story is don't tempt fate!
Place name	La Rue des Buttes St. Mary
English	Road of the mound
Where/Why?	Not much of a mound these days but presumably described the state of the road at one time.

Place name	Clos de Malerche St. Saviour
English	Difficult to plough field
Where/Why?	This road name is a mixture of Jèrriais and French which is typical of many road names in Jersey. It means piece of land at a difficult angle and/or covered in scree (mal = bad and hèrche = harrow)
Place name	Plat Douet St. Saviour
English	Flat Brook
Where/Why?	Describing the geological features of that area
Place name	La Rue du Bechet ès Cats Trinity
English	Cats' Hangout
Where/Why?	Said to be where the witches transformed themselves into cats on a Friday night (of course).

Place name	Rue de la Pierre Blanche Trinity
English	White stone
Where/Why?	It is believed that there was previously an upright white stone (standing stone or menhir) in this location.

Place name	Colin Machon St. Ouen
English	Snail
Where/Why?	A road in St. Ouen. Not a road belonging to Mr. Machon but one that is shaped somewhat like a curvy snail (colînmachon).

Place name	La Cache de Neuf Tours St. Ouen
English	The drive of nine towers
Where/Why?	Presumably so called because of the sweeping view of the defence towers built along the coastline.

Place name	Mont des Corvées St. Ouen
English	Unpleasant task hill
Where/Why?	A steep hill certainly, but not unpleasant, however perhaps the task of walking up it was!

Place name	La Rouge Tchu St. Ouen
English	The red arse
Where/Why?	Bearing in mind those from St. John were called the black arses due to sitting in their soil, perhaps the soil here was of a more red hue for sitters? This is pure conjecture however!

Place name	La Corbière St. Ouen
English	The place of the crows
Where/Why?	The location of our iconic lighthouse and some feathered-friends.
Place name	La Rue des Sillons St. Peter
English	Furrow or bank
Where/Why?	The road with furrows.

Phrases You Might Spot in St. Helier

Phrase	English	Where/Why?
L'mus est d's'y'êchanchi	Belonging is everything.	On the doors of the Co-op Charing Cross
Il n'est pon tréjous mathée quand l'baté fliotte	Just because your boat is floating, it doesn't mean the tide is in (you can't count on appearances)	Cut into the stone pavement on Conway Street
Chein tchi veint d'fliot s'en r'va d'mathée	What comes in with the tide, leaves with the tide (easy come, easy go)	Cut into the stone pavement on Conway Street
Séyiz les beinv'nus	Welcome	At Jersey port, to welcome you
Papi et magasins, tinnes et boutelles on plastique, tés	Newspapers and magazines, cans and plastic bottles, rubbish	On the bins, telling you to separate your waste
Gouvèrnément d'Jèrri	Government of Jersey	At the Government building in Broad Street

Index

Contact Us

Do you have examples of Jèrriais or other indigenous languages to share? We'd love to see them!

You can find Jèrriais Duo on social media at:
https://www.facebook.com/ Jèrriais Duo
Jèrriais-Duo@theislandofjersey

Jèrriais does not only exist in the past in Jersey, it is as much a part of the culture today as surfing, finance and agriculture – it's just not as obvious. Keep looking!

Printed in Poland
by Amazon Fulfillment
Poland Sp. z o.o., Wrocław